EFFECTIVE TEAM MEETINGS
AN OPTIMISTIC LEADER'S GUIDE

Judy Jablon

Leading for Children Publications
South Orange, NJ

Leading for Children is a non-profit organization with the mission of ensuring that every child in America has access to vibrant, high-quality early learning programs.

Copyright © 2020 by Leading for Children

All rights reserved. This book or any portion thereof may not be reproduced or used in any manner whatsoever without the express written permission of the publisher except for the use of brief quotations in a book review.

Printed in the United States of America

First Printing, 2020

Leading for Children
South Orange, NJ 07079
www.leadingforchildren.org

CONTENTS

FOREWORD
A Message from Judy Jablon 1

CHAPTER 1
The Why of Team Meetings 5

CHAPTER 2
Thinking About Optimistic Leadership 15

CHAPTER 3
The Coherent Path to Quality 23

CHAPTER 4
Structuring Team Meetings: Before, During, and After 31

CHAPTER 5
Facilitation: The Leading for Children Way 39

CHAPTER 6
Next Steps 45

Acknowledgments 49

References 51

For my colleagues,
Laura Ensler and Nichole Parks.
I'm grateful for your partnership.

FOREWORD
A MESSAGE FROM JUDY JABLON

Welcome to *Effective Team Meetings: An Optimistic Leaders Guide*. The purpose of this guide is to transform team meetings that directly or indirectly support children's learning into meaningful professional development experiences for you and the colleagues on your team. As the adults in young children's lives, we have a responsibility to ensure that they have access to high-quality early learning experiences that allow them to thrive. Think about all the meetings held in the service of children's learning, including those in: state agencies, school districts, regional organizations, and childcare programs. Adults get together to make decisions that influence children's well-being and learning. If we could transform all of these meetings into productive, collaborative learning conversations, we have a chance of ensuring equitable high-quality learning for all children.

For several years, educators who have worked with me in convenings and small group discussions have asked what they might do to make their own meetings more effective. By writing this guide, I hope that we have identified frameworks and strategies that can support each of you in shaping meetings that promote learning.

My style is to learn with and from others and for this reason I convened a group of colleagues to co-construct the content for this guide. I will refer to this amazing group of colleagues as the Development Collaborative. We met monthly to explore the challenges of typical team meetings and discuss ways to overcome them. We began by discussing the purpose of team meetings — the "why." The group agreed that effective team meetings provide opportunities for participants to:

- Learn about program priorities and news.
- Explore useful content with colleagues.
- Discover something new to put into action.
- Think about ideas in new ways.
- Apply lessons learned through their work with children, families, and each other.

Bad team meetings are like long, boring circle times in early childhood classrooms. Meeting participants have little interaction and sit too long while one or two people talk. They frequently receive irrelevant information and are exposed to a structure that fails to promote thinking and learning. I believe that team meetings in early childhood programs should mirror essential practices that are best for children. Whether a meeting is an open house for families, a faculty meeting for a group of teachers, or a team meeting for agency staff, this guide describes how to turn it into an adult professional learning opportunity that:

1 Strengthens adult-adult *relationships and interactions*,

2 Promotes healthy and productive *emotional and physical environments* for adults, and

3 Fosters *learning experiences* that lead to continuous quality improvement for children.

THREE CORE BELIEFS
AT LEADING FOR CHILDREN

Underlying our work at Leading for Children (LFC) are three core beliefs that shape our thinking and influence how we approach effective meetings.

Wisdom. Everyone has knowledge and lived experience to draw and build on while learning new skills and content and when coming together to make decisions and solve problems. Throughout our work, we acknowledge the **wisdom** of all adults, supporting them to develop trust, shared purpose, and commitment. We believe that people thrive when they feel seen and heard. By intentionally creating the conditions for all voices to be heard, we begin to achieve equity.

Team. Learning with and from each other deepens knowledge and forges strong **teams**. Together teams can collaborate to ensure continuous and sustainable quality improvement for children's early care and education.

Modeling. How adults work together **models** essential practices that support young children's brain growth and learning in all areas of development. This includes having healthy relationships and interactions, creating safe and nurturing environments, and offering effective learning experiences.

In this guide, you'll notice that we refer to elevating the **wisdom** of the group, strengthening **teams**, and using practices in team meetings that **model** best practices for children.

Let's think about what engaging meetings might look and sound like when everyone is in the same space:

LOOKS LIKE	SOUNDS LIKE
People - Are comfortable and relaxed. - Sit at tables or stand in clusters. - Move from place to place. - Smile, with eyes lit up. - Can serve themselves snacks and beverages available nearby.	People - Engage in back and forth conversation. - Laugh. - Encourage participation. - Ask and respond to questions. - Make comments.

When the team is remote, the look and sound might be a little different:

LOOKS LIKE	SOUNDS LIKE
People • May be on screen or on the phone and seated wherever they can find a quiet space. • Have prepared some water or snacks ahead of time so that they can be comfortable. • May transition from a large-group virtual meeting to a smaller breakout session. • Have unexpected visitors like pets and children.	**People** • Are speaking one person at a time. • Share laughter and smiles when something is funny. • Participate via chat, talk, polls and questions and answers. • Help family members or pets as they enter the space. • Mute themselves when there are inevitable distractions.

With these characteristics of an effective meeting in mind, the Development Collaborative experimented with the strategies we discussed in our monthly meetings. Their team meetings improved, colleagues expressed appreciation for the changes they implemented, and program practices became more consistent. Reports on how teams responded to the strategies helped us to consider the many factors involved in turning team meetings into dynamic professional learning experiences. This guide reflects the Development Collaborative's experiences, skills, and knowledge. Throughout this guide you will notice that we often refer to meeting participants as "teachers" and organizational settings as "programs." While the Development Collaborative worked most often in early learning program settings, you will find that the advice contained within can apply to any number of organizational structures and participant roles.

We've organized the guide into five chapters:

Chapter 1: The Why of Team Meetings begins with an explanation of program vision, mission, culture, and climate. Next comes a discussion of the use of team meetings as a forum for strengthening and deepening a program's vision and mission, while the content shapes the culture and climate.

Chapter 2: Thinking About Optimistic Leadership describes the critical role Optimistic Leadership plays in holding effective meetings. The Five Commitments of Optimistic Leadership are described in this chapter.

Chapter 3: The Coherent Path to Quality discusses the importance of a shared understanding of quality in creating effective meetings. The three dimensions of the Coherent Path are described in this chapter.

Chapter 4: Structuring Team Meetings: Before, During, and After takes you through the steps of organizing purposeful meetings and provides tips and strategies.

Chapter 5: Facilitation, The LFC Way introduces the idea of having a facilitative stance and presents facilitation strategies that respectfully access and elevate the wisdom of the group, strengthen teams, and model effective practices.

The book closes with some ideas for **Next Steps** — how you can implement the ideas you think will be a good fit for your setting.

One final note before moving into the book — I began Leading for Children in 2016 after almost 40 years in the early childhood field as teacher, coach, presenter, and author because I believe we can design more equitable professional learning that sustains continuous quality improvement. Leading for Children is dedicated to achieving this goal by bringing together all the adults who are part of the child's ecosystem to co-design a shared understanding of leadership and quality for young children. We include agency leaders, families, teachers, program directors, coaches, bus drivers, specialists, the kitchen team, and community partners. At Leading for Children, we believe that every adult in the child's ecosystem is a leader. Therefore, regardless of your role, I invite you to use this to ensure your meetings are inclusive, purposeful, and engaging.

On behalf of the Leading for Children team, thank you for your commitment to children, families, and educators,

Judy Jablon
Executive Director, Leading for Children

CHAPTER 1
THE WHY OF TEAM MEETINGS

Team meetings provide a space for all voices to be heard and create the opportunity for equity in your program. When the team can learn both *with* and *from* each other, strong partnerships are formed, collaboration happens, and continuous quality improvement for children is possible.

The quality of the meetings you have together is a powerful way to model how children can learn from and with each other and how families can partner with teachers on behalf of children. There are specific reasons why programs have team meetings. Our colleagues reported the following:

- Our *early learning standards* require them.
- The team members *like to get together*.
- I want to be sure *every member of the team has the same information*.
- We use team meetings to *solve problems* and *make decisions*.
- Team meetings are opportunities for *professional learning*.

Early childhood team meetings address all the purposes listed above with professional learning at the forefront. Team meetings are likely to address specific **content** such as the need to:

- Meet licensing requirements, such as reviewing child abuse and neglect reporting requirements.
- Address professional development requests noted in team surveys, such as family conferences, working effectively together in teaching teams, and time management.
- Enhance practices identified as in need of attention, such as offering a variety of activities and experiences during outdoor play times.
- Work on specific goals such as establishing family-style dining in all classrooms.

As you plan team meetings as opportunities for professional learning, align them with your program's vision and mission. How you engage team in thinking together creates the program's culture — the beliefs and values shared within the learning community. The climate of your program — the feelings people have when they spend time in the setting — is also shaped by team meetings. Cohesion comes from the alignment of vision, mission, culture, and climate, and team meetings can help you achieve it. For this reason, we discuss vision, mission, culture, and climate in detail in this chapter and illustrate how each connects with team meetings.

The Vision & Mission of Your Program

One key purpose of working together as a team is to strengthen and deepen the *why* of your program — your program's vision and mission. Effective team meetings support open communication, allowing the team to reflect, plan, and strategize together. This is a necessary step in ensuring that your shared vision and mission are realized. While this book is not primarily about vision and mission, let's look at some simple definitions as they relate to team meetings.

Vision. The vision reflects the program's hope for children's futures. It is a north star—an anchor—for the work you and the team do every day. Consider these questions:

- Does your program have a vision statement?[1]
- Does it align with your thinking about child development, responding to the needs of individual children and families, equity, diversity, and inclusion?
- Does your team know what the program's vision is? How do you know they are or are not committed to the vision?
- How do others know the program's vision? Is it in your brochure? On your website? In materials for families? In job descriptions?

Team meetings are a perfect time to invite the team to reflect on the why of your program. It could be a brief item on every meeting agenda or covered in depth in a series of meetings. Regardless, the content of the team meeting should always be tied to the vision of the program. The more obvious and transparent the vision is, the more likely it is that people will understand, respect, and embrace it.

Throughout this chapter we will use an example of a fictional program we are calling The Oak Grove School to show how mission and vision can (and should) play a role in meeting planning.

---

[1] If your program or organization does not have a vision statement, it is time to form an inclusive work group to create one.

Aligning the Vision Statement with Team Meeting Topics

The Oak Grove School's vision statement is "All children feel safe, cared for, respected, and encouraged to develop to their fullest potential." A topic in this week's staff meeting is respecting children's accomplishments. The following table is an example that shows how the meeting planner can ensure that her meeting discussion is aligned with the program's vision.

VISION STATEMENT	All children feel safe, cared for, respected, and encouraged to develop to their fullest potential.
TEAM MEETING TOPIC	Respecting Children's Accomplishments
DISCUSSION PROMPTS & QUESTIONS	In what ways do we validate children's successes? Share a story of a recent experience during which you encouraged a child to take a step towards learning something new.
ALIGNMENT	

The meeting topic aligns with the program's vision.

Participants:

- identify specific strategies they use to validate children.
- share stories about how they help children make progress.

Throughout this chapter we will continue to build on this example.

Mission. A mission statement guides the day-to-day work of an organization. Most likely your program has a mission statement that describes the steps taken to achieve the vision. Review the mission of your program and reflect on how it aligns with the vision and your own thinking. If there isn't alignment, consider creating a work group to address this issue. If there is alignment, invite the team to think about how the vision and mission support your work with children and families.

When a team has a shared understanding of the mission and vision of the organization, it is as if everyone is singing in harmony from the same song sheet. In conversations with colleagues around the country, we often hear about misalignment within a program. For example, one team member thinks each classroom should set their own policy about serving snack while another firmly believes that consistency in snack policy from one classroom to the next is vital. At another program, some teachers do not want to take their children on field trips while others firmly believe in neighborhood excursions that help children to learn about the community. Thus, their classrooms, interactions, and curriculum are designed to achieve different goals. When each person has a personal song sheet it creates dissonance and can be an underlying factor when team meetings are ineffective.

For children and families to thrive in a program, the team needs to embrace coherence of vision and mission — the overall purpose or why of the work. Coherence means that everything fits together in an organized and consistent manner. We will discuss this topic in more detail in *Chapter 3: The Coherent Path to Quality*.

Take a moment to think about the alignment between vision and mission in the chart on the next page. Note that the mission statement is more specific and actionable.

Aligning Program Mission with Team Meeting Topics

The Oak Grove School's mission statement is "We ensure that all members of our program community have open, honest, trusting, and two-way relationships and interactions in an emotional and physical environment that is safe, calm, organized and respectful so that children and adults can have learning experiences that are meaningful, exploratory and actionable." A topic in this week's staff meeting is Building Reciprocal and Trusting Family Partnerships. The following table is an example that shows how the meeting planner can ensure that her meeting discussion is aligned with the program's vision and mission.

VISION	All young children feel safe, loved, respected and encouraged to develop to their fullest potential.
MISSION	We ensure that all members of our program community have open, honest, trusting, and two-way relationships and interactions in an emotional and physical environment that is safe, calm, organized and respectful so that children and adults can have learning experiences that are meaningful, exploratory and actionable.* *Derived from *The Coherent Path to Quality*
MEETING TOPIC	Building Reciprocal and Trusting Family Partnerships
DISCUSSION PROMPTS & QUESTIONS	To explore this topic, let's discuss: • How do we define trust? • What do we do to promote reciprocal trusting relationships with families? • What other strategies can we try?
ALIGNMENT	

How is the program's mission aligned with the meeting topic?

- The team will create a shared understanding of trust.
- They will share wisdom about ways they build reciprocal trusting partnerships with families.
- They will develop new ways to enhance family partnerships.

Clarity about vision and mission bring the team together around a common purpose. Two other important aspects of the organization are the program's culture and climate.

Think About the Culture & Climate of Your Program

Vision and mission define the direction of your program. Culture and climate are a guide to enacting the vision and mission. The following definitions illustrate how culture and climate influence the effectiveness and value of team meetings.

Defining Program Culture

Bloom and Abel define the culture of an early childhood setting as what makes it unique:

> Culture includes the shared values, assumptions, and collective beliefs about what is important, and the norms and expectations for what is appropriate and acceptable in everyday interactions. Culture also includes the traditions, rituals, celebrations, and customs that distinguish one program or school from another. [2]

Is it an assumption and belief that children and adults are supported and respected at your program? Do you share a belief that all voices must be heard and that equity, diversity, and inclusion are vital to the learning environment? Do all team members accept their roles as leaders for children? Do you believe that strong, trusting relationships among adults and with children are the foundation for learning? All of these are examples of program culture.

Sometimes a program's culture is *implicit* — not spelled out in writing or spoken of regularly. This can cause friction among the team. New team members typically try to figure out what the culture or "rules" are for fitting in and being successful. For example, every year at Spring Hill Preschool teachers and families organize a fall festival that takes place on the second Saturday in October. For the two weeks prior, everyone pitches in extra hours to ensure a successful event that raises funds for the program. This year two recently-hired teachers asked about additional compensation for the extra hours of work involved. The meeting facilitator and veteran teachers were annoyed that these newcomers would ask the question. The two teachers felt ostracized for what seemed to them a reasonable question. The implicit culture of the program was to go the extra mile on behalf of the program. However, for the two new teachers, this was not discussed during their interviews or onboarding process. Now they felt upset about being expected to work additional unpaid time and resented participation in the fall festival. Tension among team members grew. This exemplifies the risks of an implicit culture

In contrast, consider this example where the culture is explicit. At Parkway Early Childhood Center, Ms. Rodriquez, the Meeting Facilitator, introduces the program's culture during hiring interviews. She tells candidates about the importance of family engagement and how throughout the year there will be activities on some evenings and weekends. She further explains how salaries are based on inclusion of additional work hours. In this way newly-hired teachers are clear about expectations from beginning. These expectations are also clarified in the team handbook.

Try using various forums including family gatherings and team meetings to hold explicit conversation about culture. Team members who have been at the school for thirty years may have different assumptions than new teachers just coming on board. The more explicit you make the culture, the healthier the climate will be and team meetings will be more successful.

---

[2] P.J. Bloom and M. Abel. 2015. "Expanding the Lens—Leadership as an Organizational Asset." *Young Children* 70, no. 2 (May 2015), https://www.naeyc.org/resources/pubs/yc/may2015/expanding-the-lens.

Aligning the Program's Culture with Team Meetings

Let's assume that in our example, the Oak Grove School culture values the importance of strong, respectful relationships among adults to support strong, positive relationships and interactions between adults and children. Given the vision, mission, and program culture, let's look how they can ensure these are reflected in their team meeting.

VISION	All young children feel safe, loved, respected and encouraged to develop to their fullest potential.
MISSION	We ensure that all members of our program community have open, honest, trusting, and two-way relationships and interactions in an emotional and physical environment that is safe, calm, organized and respectful so that children and adults can have learning experiences that are meaningful, exploratory and actionable.
PROGRAM CULTURE	We are all leaders for children who build and sustain trusting relationships.
MEETING STRUCTURE	• A few team members help develop the agenda. • The agenda is distributed at least two days before the meeting. • 10 minutes of each meeting is allocated for open discussion.

ALIGNMENT

The structure of the meeting aligns with the programs culture, vision and mission in that:

- Roles and responsibilities are shared.

- The agenda is distributed in advance to demonstrate respect and to offer people time to reflect on the content prior to the meeting.

- The slide show demonstrates respect and appreciation and the sharing conveys that every voice matters.

- If the meeting is face to face, the room arrangement is conducive to interactions and materials and space are organized to support respectful group thinking and sharing.

- If the meeting is remote, be sure to provide time for small group conversations.

Defining Program Climate

The climate in a program is what it feels like to there. A recent study of early learning program climate identified the following characteristics: collegiality, professional development, meeting facilitator support, clarity, reward system, decision making, goal consensus, task orientation, physical setting, and innovativeness.[3] How would you describe your program climate in terms of these characteristics?

The climate among adults significantly influences how children and families feel when they enter the program. When the climate is healthy, safe, and respectful, and team members value supporting one another and learning together, children and families feel comfortable. In addition, in this kind of climate, team meetings are likely to be vibrant and engaging.

---

[3] Veziroglu-Celik, M & T. Yildiz . 2018 . "Organizational Climate in Early Childhood Education." *Journal of Education and Training Studies.* 6. 88. 10.11114/jets.v6i12.3698.

How Climate Affects Team Meetings

The Oak Grove School has worked hard to achieve a climate that is respectful, equitable, and inclusive. Let's look at how this is reflected in their meeting structure.

VISION	All young children feel safe, loved, respected and encouraged to develop to their fullest potential.
MISSION	We ensure that all members of our program community have open, honest, trusting, and two-way relationships and interactions in an emotional and physical environment that is safe, calm, organized and respectful so that children and adults can have learning experiences that are meaningful, exploratory and actionable.
PROGRAM CULTURE	We are all leaders for children who build and sustain trusting relationships.
CLIMATE	Respectful, equitable, and inclusive.
MEETING STRUCTURE	• The meeting begins with a two-minute slide show that highlights each team member engaged in an effective teacher-child interaction. • The meeting facilitator invites everyone to jot down a word or phrase that comes to mind as they watch the slides. • Next, the meeting facilitator invites each person to greet the team and share the word or phrase they wrote to convey that every voice matters.
ALIGNMENT	

Implications for the program's climate and team meetings include:

- All team members' strengths are highlighted through the slideshow
- All team members are seen and heard.
- Time is allocated for individual responses.

Team meetings create cohesion in your program and ensure that everyone is singing from the same song sheet. Use your program's vision and mission as a resource to help you achieve cohesion. As you choose topics for team meetings, align them with the vision and mission. In the next chapter, we will talk about how the Five Commitments of Optimistic Leadership[4] can support you in promoting a healthy and positive program culture and climate.

---

[4] Judy Jablon. "The Five Commitments of Optimistic Leadership." *Exchange* (November/December 2018): 26-30.

CHAPTER 2
THINKING ABOUT OPTIMISTIC LEADERSHIP

We know that young children thrive in an environment of trusting relationships with the adults who care for and educate them. All aspects of children's development — intellectual, social, emotional, physical, behavioral, and moral — are shaped by the relationships they have with the adults in their lives. Imagine an environment of nurturing relationships where every adult in children's lives owns a clear sense of purpose, has a strong voice, and listens and learns from diverse perspectives. These adults are intentional decision-makers who collaborate with others to make good things happen. They are optimistic, see a path forward, and have the grit to persevere even when the going gets tough. Consider the possibilities for all children if they could live and learn in an environment with such exemplary models of leadership surrounding them. Optimistic Leaders can work together in team meetings to learn with and from each other and make decisions efficiently and effectively.

Optimists are hopeful and confident about the future or the successful outcome of something. Optimistic Leaders are passionate about achieving a vision and will persevere even when challenges impede progress. Imagine what might happen if everyone in your setting embraced his or her role as an Optimistic Leader committed to working together so all children have opportunities to be successful learners?

Leading for Children (LFC) defines leadership as owning the impact you have on others. For a director, this might mean how you interact with your team to inspire their professionalism. For a teacher, this could mean the way you ignite curiosity in children and welcome families as partners in their children's learning. Leaders inspire others to work towards a common goal — the vision and mission of your early learning program.

What does commitment mean to you? A definition that we can all relate to is *commitment means staying loyal to what you said you were going to do even after the mood you said it in passes.* For example, does this director's story ring a familiar bell?

After reading an article about the benefits of yoga, Devora signs up for a yoga class that meets every Tuesday morning at 6:15am. For a few weeks she enthusiastically attends, but then the inspiration of the article fades and sleeping in for the extra thirty minutes on Tuesdays instead of going to yoga prevails. Devora's commitment dissipates. When a friend invites her to join a different yoga class a few months later, Devora agrees and recommits to her wellness plan.

Leading for Children (LFC) uses the *Five Commitments of Optimistic Leadership* to help early childhood educators be more effective in their day-to-day work. The descriptions below illustrate how the five commitments work together to achieve a common goal.

❶ **Think Impact** to make informed decisions. Everything we do and say — all of our actions — has consequences or benefits. Too often we are on auto-pilot or rushing from one thing to the next. Whether you are writing an email, making a phone call, or welcoming participants to a team meeting, take a moment to ask yourself: What do I want to happen? Then, consider the behaviors, actions, and words that will be most effective in achieving the desired result. For a team meeting, for example, you might invite team members to take turns facilitating the opening activity with the goal of providing opportunities to be creative and to practice leading a group, as they might do when holding a classroom family night.

❷ **Cultivate Self-Awareness** to guide thought, emotion, and behavior. Self-awareness includes the ability to think about how others see you and to consider the perspectives of others. As you plan your actions and words, first assess your mood, fatigue, and feelings towards others. Ask yourself: Am I willing to accommodate their needs and emotions? During the meeting, for example, you might let go of the agenda you planned when you realize that teachers want to share previous family conference successes and challenges with each other.

❸ **Nurture Relationships** to support learning and collaboration. We learn best through strong, trusting connections with colleagues, families, and children. Although some professional relationships do not come naturally, we can learn and use strategies to navigate them. Research shows the importance of high-quality trusting relationships in achieving positive educational outcomes[5]. For example, Miss Sharmaine, an experienced toddler teacher, knows that families in her program have varied views about toilet training. To ensure strong partnerships with each family, she works closely with them to discuss and agree upon the strategy that be best for each child.

❹ **Refine Communication** for mutual clarity and understanding. Communication is key to maintaining positive and effective relationships. It includes listening, speaking, writing, and being keenly aware of non-verbal communication—your own and that of others. Think about conscious and unconscious word choices, tone of voice, and non-verbal signals you project. Are they supporting or hampering effective communication? For example, what might you say and do to let team meeting participants know that their input is relevant? "Takima, I noticed several of your team members nodding as you told us how you take time to greet every child and family, every day."

❺ **Activate Curiosity** to find connections and continue learning. Through curiosity we are more willing to take risks, experiment, and try something new. To keep an open mind, use curiosity rather than judgment to navigate your role as leader. You can ask genuine questions and convey a sense of wonder rather than worry or doubt. Consider this example. During a discussion of rest time in the weekly team meeting, Raashan asserts that he doesn't allow children to bring books to their cots. Program director, Sonja, firmly disagrees with him but doesn't want a confrontation. Instead she activates curiosity by inviting the group to reflect together by saying: "Let's list considerations that help us make intentional decisions about rest time practices." The group begins to brainstorm as Sonja charts their ideas. By the end of this discussion, many ideas about rest time have surfaced and she feels comfortable waiting to talk with Raashan about his views at a later time, knowing that the group conversation had given him food for thought about his no-books rule.

---

[5] M. Wechsler, H. Melnick, A. Maier, and J. Bishop. *The Building Blocks of High-Quality Early Childhood Education Program*. (Policy brief, Learning Policy Institute, 2016), 2.

Think about what it means to you to embrace your role as an Optimistic Leader. Optimistic Leaders strive to embody the *Five Commitments of Optimistic Leadership* and apply them in every aspect of program planning and operations, including team meetings. Think about your actions as ripples on a pond — using one practice has multiple outcomes. The more clarity you build about each of these commitments the more progress you will make towards having engaging and productive team meetings.

You can use *the Five Commitments of Optimistic Leadership* as a reflection tool to support you in planning and implementing team meetings. You will also find a discussion of how to use the Five Commitments of Optimistic Leadership to create group norms for team meetings in Chapter 5.

Questions to Consider for Team Meetings

Use the Five Commitments of Optimistic Leadership Leaders to inspire you and your team to achieve the best possible program for the children and families you serve. When you reflect on each commitment, it is a way to ensure that you are intentional in your decisions and actions.

COMMITMENT	**Think Impact** *to make informed decisions*
REFLECTIVE QUESTIONS	Think about the impact you want the meeting to have on the team: • What knowledge do you hope team members gain? • Do you want them to be more confident as learners and leaders for children? • Will they be motivated to take initiative and put new ideas into action?
YOUR REFLECTIONS	

COMMITMENT	**Cultivate Self-Awareness** *to guide thought, emotion, and behavior*
REFLECTIVE QUESTIONS	Reflect on your thoughts and feelings about the purpose of the meeting: • What emotions does it raise for you? • Are you invested in this content, somewhat bored by it, or need to do some research to help you prepare? • Might others think with you so you can consider multiple perspectives? • Is a meeting needed at all, or would it be more productive to send the information via email?
YOUR REFLECTIONS	

Thinking About Optimistic Leadership

COMMITMENT	**Nurture Relationships** *to support learning and collaboration*
REFLECTIVE QUESTIONS	Think about how the meeting can strengthen relationships with you and among the team: • How can you foster each participant's success with the experience? • What might you do to ensure the experience supports your relationship with each person? • Would it be beneficial to create different groupings to invite new partnerships?

YOUR REFLECTIONS

COMMITMENT	**Refine Communication** *for mutual clarity and understanding*
REFLECTIVE QUESTIONS	Think about how your communication style affects the team's receptivity to the experience. • How can you use communication to set everyone up for success? • How can you mediate your tone and choice of words as you offer invitations and reminders?

YOUR REFLECTIONS

COMMITMENT	**Activate Curiosity** *to find connections and continue learning*
REFLECTIVE QUESTIONS	Think about how you use curiosity and inspire it in others: - Do you tend to make statements more than you ask questions? - Are the questions you ask open-ended? - Are you so passionate about the topic that you want to tell the group everything? - Would it help to invite a few people to think with you about questions that allow creative exploration from diverse perspectives?

YOUR REFLECTIONS

CHAPTER 3
THE COHERENT PATH TO QUALITY

In Chapter 1, we established that the purpose of working together as a team is to strengthen and deepen the *why* of the work, and throughout the guide our premise has been that our why is to ensure that all children have high-quality early learning experiences. Too often, the vision of high quality varies from person to person. Think about the people in your team meetings. Are they all singing from the same song sheet in terms of program quality?

To support programs in gaining alignment, Leading for Children (LFC) has developed a framework called *The Coherent Path to Quality*. The framework defines three dimensions of program quality: relationships and interactions, the emotional and physical environment, and learning experiences. Each dimension has "simple rules" or criteria for establishing shared understanding and for ensuring all children and adults thrive. These rules are a "package" — you can't just pick the ones you like.

Our goal in creating this framework is to make the concept of high quality for all children user-friendly: *"concrete and specific"* so that all adults who work with children and families can grasp what it means, why it matters, and how to implement it. We also believe that this framework applies to adults as well as children.

You read about the three tenets of Leading for Children: wisdom, team and modeling. In this chapter we share the Coherent Path to Quality as a tool that you can use in two ways to support your team in having a shared vision of quality. First, you can use it to guide your planning because you model high quality practices in how you facilitate team meetings. Second, you can incorporate aspects of it as topics for discussion.

PROGRAM QUALITY

1. Relationships & Interactions
2. The Emotional & Physical Environment
3. Learning Experiences

The framework defines three dimensions of program quality: relationships and interactions, the emotional and physical environment, and learning experiences.

COHERENT PATH TO QUALITY

RELATIONSHIPS & INTERACTIONS
HONEST | TRUSTING | OPEN | TWO-WAY

EMOTIONAL & PHYSICAL ENVIRONMENT
CALM | SAFE | ORGANIZED | RESPECTFUL

LEARNING EXPERIENCES
MEANINGFUL | EXPLORATORY | ACTIONABLE

IMPROVING OUTCOMES FOR CHILDREN

Dimension #1
Relationships & Interactions

Take a moment to think about how you feel when you are with someone. Relaxed? Comfortable? Safe? Edgy? Displaced? Defensive? In our work in early learning, relationships and interactions matter because they affect how we — children and adults — think, feel, and learn.

How adults relate to and interact with each other offers young children the most powerful model for how to be with others. Team meetings are an essential format for promoting strong, positive relationships and interactions among adults. In the next chapter you will find many strategies for promoting positive relationships and interactions as you plan meetings.

When the relationships and interactions are healthy and strong among the adults in the child's life, the emotional climate supports a child's well-being. Most importantly, children develop and learn within the context of strong positive relationships and interactions with the adults who care for them. Here are some simple rules to guide our decisions about relationships and interactions:

1. **Honest.** *Honesty means telling the truth. An honest relationship is "real" — it is authentic and genuine. Interactions are honest when they are sincere — they come from the heart.*

2. **Trusting.** *Trust is a feeling that develops in response to the actions and words of a person. When you trust someone, you know they will be there for you, they will support you and you can rely on them. Over time, a person's honesty allows you to trust them.*

3. **Open.** *Being open means you convey (with your body language, words and actions) to others that they are welcome to be with you, to interact with you. You are friendly and approachable.*

4. **Two-way.** *A two-way relationship is equitable — each person is respected and valued. It is balanced so that both people feel seen and heard. In a two-way relationship or interaction, there is mutuality and reciprocity.*

Dimension #2
Emotional & Physical Environment

Think about how you feel when you enter a room — does it stress you out? Make you anxious? Relax you? Help you calm down? The emotional and physical environment matters because it affects how we feel, how we relate to others, and our ability to focus on tasks.

The emotional and physical environment of a meeting, whether face to face or remote, affects everyone's mood and the effectiveness of the experience. People thrive when the emotional and physical environment has been prepared with intention. The emotional climate of a program helps children feel safe and in turn, increases positive behavior. A healthy emotional climate reduces children's absenteeism and team turnover. When families enter an early childhood program and feel welcomed, they are more comfortable and secure leaving the child so that they can go about the business of their day. When team comes to work, the environment should motivate them to have a productive and satisfying day. Here are some simple rules to guide decisions about the emotional and physical environment:

1. **Safe.** *Safe means that people, adults and children are emotionally, physically and mentally protected from discomfort and danger. The environment is intentionally designed to ensure children are visible at all times so that they can work independently but at the same time, be easily supervised by adults.*

2. **Calm.** *When an environment is calm-it soothes your senses. Smells are pleasant and not overpowering. Visually it appeals to the eyes and invite you relax and take in the atmosphere. You hear sounds of laughter and conversations without it being overstimulating or intrusive. This calmness in the environment supports self-regulation as well as resiliency. It sends the message: "you're in a safe place to explore and follow your curiosity."*

3. **Organized.** *The physical environment presents an immediate message of either belonging or exclusion. It can provide opportunities for success and mastery, or failure and boring repetition. It can provide an arrangement of space and materials so that children can be independent, or it can be set up where teachers are the "material brokers." It can provide spaces and activities for developing community, or be so noisy, crowded, and chaotic that this is impossible.*

4. **Respectful.** *The environment makes parents and guardians feel welcome, involved, and empowered. The physical environment presents an immediate message of either belonging or exclusion. They are places where learners feel at home. In surroundings where students are willing to open their minds and actually listen to what you have to say, you can empower them to achieve their highest potential.*

Dimension #3
Learning Experiences

Think about a time you learned something new. Your curiosity was sparked and you enjoyed yourself. How would you describe your experience? Did it feel like it was connected to something of interest to you? Did you get to independently explore and answer questions? Will you be able to use what you learned? Team meetings are opportunities to learn with and from others. How you shape the meeting is a model for effective learning experiences.

When learning experiences are meaningful, they have been intentionally developed with the learner in mind. We're better able to learn new skills and knowledge when it connects to something we know a little about: our cultural and social context, our interests and goals. High quality learning experiences invite the learner to explore and construct by connecting the familiar with something new that the person can use purposefully. We invite you to think together with your team about these simple rules and have a discussion to articulate learning experiences that are effective for children.

1 **Meaningful.** When learning experiences are meaningful, they connect to something familiar to the learner. It has meaning and value to the learner. The new learning offers a small stretch rather than a huge leap beyond the learner's capability.

2 **Exploratory.** Exploratory learning experiences spark the curiosity of the learner. While it is relevant to what is familiar, it's new enough to invite investigation and wonder. The learner begins to build questions and seek answers. What will happen if I? How does this work? Why does it work that way?

3 **Actionable.** When learning experiences are actionable, the learner can see how to use what she has learned and easily use new learning for a purpose.

Use the Coherent Path to Quality to help you think about planning and as a helpful organizer for shaping more productive team meetings.

DIMENSION #1	**Relationships & Interactions**
REFLECTIVE QUESTIONS	Think about ways you can promote positive relationships and interactions in team meetings: • When you think about your team, what stands out about their connections to each other? How do you build on these connections and strengthen new ones? • What are some ways you can allow team members time to greet one another and socialize in a way that is included in the meeting's agenda? • How do you create opportunities for paired or small group work that encourages conversation and sharing ideas? • In what ways do you model inclusive behavior that promotes collegiality and limits workplace gossip? • Has everyone who should be in the meeting been invited? If someone is missing, do you acknowledge their absence?

YOUR REFLECTIONS

The Coherent Path to Quality

DIMENSION #2

Emotional & Physical Environment

REFLECTIVE QUESTIONS

Think about ways you can shape the emotional and physical environment in team meetings:

- What are some ways you create a warm and welcoming environment?

- If refreshments are being served, have you considered dietary restrictions so that everyone is comfortable?

- In what ways do you plan the space so that team members can see and hear one another?

- How do you ensure that meeting participation is inclusive?

- What are some ways you navigate disagreement so that everyone can continue to actively participate even when tension occurs?

YOUR REFLECTIONS

DIMENSION #3	Learning Experiences
REFLECTIVE QUESTIONS	Think about the learning experiences you can include in team meetings: • What prior knowledge do team members have about the topic and do you recognize and validate it? • In what ways do you ensure that you stretching the thinking of your team members? • What are you doing to elevate the wisdom of the room? • How are you making this experience engaging? • How are you going to ensure this meeting leads to your team creating actionable experiences in the classroom or with their own teams?

YOUR REFLECTIONS

As you read the next chapter, you will find more ideas about how to model the dimensions of the Coherent Path to Quality in team meetings.

CHAPTER 4
STRUCTURING TEAM MEETINGS: BEFORE, DURING & AFTER

Effective team meetings become meaningful, exploratory and actionable learning experiences for everyone involved when they address planned objectives and promote active participation. Planning includes the content of the meeting (what people will learn) as well as the process (what people will do to think, talk, and learn together). In the same way that we encourage teachers to *think impact* by being intentional and reflective, we encourage you to model these practices when planning team meetings. A good plan allows you to be fully present so you can connect with team members and facilitate responsively. During team meetings you are a model for how teachers show up and cast a shadow each day with children and families.

Before Team Meetings

As you plan for each team meeting, consider three components: purpose, content, and process.

1 **Purpose.** The purpose might be to think expansively about an issue or problem and come to a solution. Or, it could be to learn something new, exchange strategies, or prepare for upcoming family conferences. Model intentionality by being clear about what you hope the group can accomplish. When you are clear about the purpose, you can then consider how to frame the content.

2 **Content**. The topic of the meeting is the content. As you choose topics, determine how they correspond to the vision and mission of your organization.

3 **Process**. The process is the *how* of team meetings — what you do to *nurture relationships*, *refine communication* and *activate curiosity* among team members. Use the facilitation methods described in Chapter 5 to ensure that team members can share and expand their ideas and describe specific teaching strategies. *Think impact* as you plan to introduce segments, implement transitions, highlight connections, and summarize the meeting. What questions and prompts might facilitate the team to think more deeply and clarify their ideas? Plan for the three dimensions of the Coherent Path to Quality:

   — trusting, open, honest and two-way relationships and interactions;

   — a safe, calm, organized and respectful emotional and physical environment; and

   — meaningful learning experiences that allow participants to explore and apply learning.

Before: Planning the Agenda

Being clear and transparent about the planned agenda for each team meeting will enhance team engagement. As you think about each meeting's purpose—in addition to the standard information sharing you do—be sure to anchor it in your program's vision and mission (see Chapter 1). When sharing the meeting's purpose with others, articulate why the topic matters to team, children, and families. Here are tips for preparing the team meeting agenda:

- **Clarify the goal.** Participants should know why they are there so they can offer their best selves to the group. If you explain the goal in advance, team members have a better chance of arriving prepared to take part.

- **Include only relevant items in the agenda.** Be a good steward of time and energy and focus on essential topics. Harvard Business Review writer, Paul Axtell, suggests: "As a target, put 20% fewer items on your agenda and allow 20% more time for each item."[6] Consider this: if it can be said in your weekly email update, it does not need to be in a meeting. Save your time for voices, not announcements. (On the other hand, try to combine messages in a single email so people know it is important and will make time to read it.) If you are concerned that some team members may not be attentive enough to messages conveyed via email, begin the meeting by asking: "Are there any comments or questions about the recent email update?"

- **Send the agenda before the meeting.** An agenda sent out three days ahead of the meeting gives staff members time to think about how they might contribute, but not too much time for them to forget. It also conveys trust in them to think constructively about the topic. Finally, it shows that you want to make the best use of your time with one another. Some leaders worry that sending an agenda in advance can trigger negativity from staff who find certain topics challenging or frustrating. If that is a concern, look back at the Five Commitments of Optimistic Leadership and use them to help you address potential resistance before the meeting.

- **Include estimated time frames.** Use the agenda as a reliable guide. Stay present and responsible to ensure that the purpose is accomplished and that any adjustments that might need to be made are decided upon together with the group's input.

- **Prepare engaging materials.** Think about how you want the team to explore content during the meeting. You might create an interesting handout, use a blog post from the web, or print copies of a short article. The materials you prepare serve as the grist for sharing, discussing, solving problems, and posing questions.

---

[6] Paul Axtell, "How to Design Meetings Your Team Will Want to Attend," Harvard Business Review, April 5, 2017, https://hbr.org/2017/04/how-to-design-meetings-your-team-will-want-to-attend.

Before: Planning the Environment

Recall our discussion of the emotional and physical environment. As you plan a meeting, think about location, seating, and groupings if the meeting is face-to-face. If the meeting is remote, consider how you will ensure that it is safe and respectful for everyone. One program director switched her meetings from a classroom — where meetings had been held for as long as she could remember — to a space where everyone could sit around a large table and see one another. With this single change to the meeting format she reported greater team participation, with everyone seeming to be more engaged and relaxed. Later, team members gave her feedback about how much they appreciated the new setting. Just as we think about the environment and arrangement of furniture for children, we need to do the same when planning to facilitate conversations among adults. If the group is going to do small group work, then clusters of tables and chairs is best. If it is mostly large group interaction, then it is important for everyone to see one another. You can vary how participants choose their seats. Sometimes people sit where they choose, while other times you create groupings that allow for diverse perspectives in discussion.

REMOTE MEETINGS
PLANNING THE ENVIRONMENT

When planning for remote meetings, it's vital to be intentional about how the group can connect and interact when everyone is in different spaces, some people may be on the phone while others are on video. Simple considerations can be helpful:

- Allow time and be patient with technology issues. Some people need more time to figure out how to come off mute, others may have background noise that they can't control, and some may be on the phone while others are on video.

- Be sensitive to "names" as not everyone has their device set up only for their use. People may be using phones that have the name of their device. Others may be sharing a computer with family members or want to protect confidentiality.

- Consider using virtual backgrounds if there is sensitivity about sharing where you are.

During Team Meetings

As you implement your meeting plan, remember you are modeling for the team how you expect they will assist and communicate with each other, support children and families, and interact in a group meeting. It can be hard to manage your schedule so there is a break between your last appointment and the beginning of team meetings. However, if you come in rushing from something else, or you are late, think about the shadow that casts. It's critical that you are fully present.

Arrive early to prepare the space, leaving time to connect with individuals as they arrive. If you use a classroom space, work with the classroom team to set it up so that everyone can see one another. Put materials on tables ahead of time. If snacks will be provided, decide where they will be placed and set up them up in advance.

Think about modeling. Your greeting of each team member is like the greeting teachers do with children and families each day. Convey to each person that you see and hear them and that they matter.

A successful meeting has a clear beginning, the work time, and a summative conclusion. Careful planning allows you to consider timing and flow.

> **REMOTE MEETINGS**
> **DURING TEAM MEETINGS**
>
> It is just as important to arrive early as host of a virtual meeting so that you can greet people as they arrive, support them with feeling comfortable and help them with technology.

The Beginning

As an Optimistic Leader, how you begin a meeting matters! Start on time! Waiting for stragglers sets the tone that being late is okay and that those who came on time are less important. Think about *nurturing relationships* by welcoming team members to the meeting and encouraging them to shift gears. Acknowledge the importance of taking a breath and quieting the *static* (see box, below).

For mutual clarity, articulate the meeting's purpose, its connection to the program vision and mission, and how it is responsive to the program's movement on the path to quality. Review the main agenda segments for the meeting.

The Five Commitments of Optimistic Leadership are an effective tool to shape group norms. Using group norms in meetings provides a solid basis for getting the most out of the meeting and promotes mutual accountability and responsibility among the group. Just as we encourage teachers to engage children in thinking about classroom rules or expectations, it is imperative to engage your team in thinking about team meeting expectations. In the box to the right, you will find each commitment and a few reflective questions to support the practice of the commitment.

Begin with an experience that sets the tone. In Chapter 5 we will introduce a Leading for Children facilitation technique called the Carousel Share that ensures all voices are heard and promotes engagement from the beginning.

GROUP NORMS
THE FIVE COMMITMENTS OF OPTIMISTIC LEADERS

Think Impact. Before you act or speak, pause and prepare to listen. As you listen and prepare to respond, ask yourself: am I reacting or have I taken time to reflect?

Cultivate Self-Awareness. Ask yourself, how am I showing up today? Am I fully present? Think about what you want to do to be your best self.

Nurture Relationships. Ask yourself, what am I doing to strengthen my relationships with others? How am I supporting the relationships in my group?

Refine Communication. Ask yourself, am I being mindful of my spoken words? How is my tone? Am I listening to others' ideas and taking the time to understand and evaluate in order to learn? What kind of feedback am I giving and is it strength-based? Am I aware of everyone's visual cues?

Activate Curiosity. Ask yourself, am I staying open to learn today or am I simply stating my beliefs over and over again? Am I noticing connections between previous thoughts and new ideas?

POWERFUL INTERACTIONS
QUIET THE STATIC

In the book *Powerful Interactions* the authors describe "pausing to quiet the static."[7] Static is defined as the noise in your head that interferes with your ability to focus on something.

---

[7] A. Dombro, J. Jablon, and C. Stetson. *Powerful Interactions: How to Connect with Children to Extend Their Learning.* (Washington, D.C.: NAEYC, 2011), 13.

The Work Time

Whether you have 15 or 90 minutes to work, make sure it is meaningful, exploratory, and actionable. Shape the discussion topics in a way that allows every person in the room to understand their role. If the topic is family conferences, and you have a physical education and art teacher present, think in advance of how they can contribute to the discussion. For example, their input is needed so classroom teachers can share it during family conferences.

During the work time, invite people to think together. Include time for investigation through problem solving, questioning, discussing, brainstorming, and exchange of strategies.

Remain mindful of the main idea or objective for each segment, and of the timing. Refer to the agenda often. This helps the group to stay focused on the purpose and content. It also promotes shared ownership of the agenda and outcomes.

Finally, allow time during this segment to encourage each person to translate the exploration into action. How will they apply the ideas discussed?

With the group, capture decisions and action items, pushing for specificity. For example, record group ideas, responses, and/or questions on chart paper so they can see their words. This is a way of navigating and encouraging all voices, reflecting their wisdom back to them, and building on each other's thinking together. In addition, take notes during the discussion, capturing key words and ideas, circling those that stand out, and restating people's contributions back to the group. This helps group members to experience your transparency about what you are documenting, to hear how their contributions matter, and to see what documenting together looks like.

Summative Conclusion

Be sure to leave a few minutes at the end to review the session and establish next steps with the team. You might:

- invite each person to share one action to implement immediately,
- share items from your notes that will help the group apply what they learned,
- agree to continue the discussion in the next meeting,
- form a small group to plan a follow-up meeting, and
- ask for a volunteer who will type up and disseminate the charts created.

One thing that many directors reported about problematic meetings is how discussions end up in a black hole! Bring closure to the meeting so that everyone knows that the purpose of the meeting has been met and that there are clear actions to take as a result of the time spent together.

After Team Meetings

How you follow up and communicate about your actions after a meeting lets your team know that you are trustworthy leader who does what you say you will do and that you honor their contributions and requests. By showing that the work you do together matters, you build motivation and openness and contribute to a supportive and optimistic culture and climate in your program. This taps into existing trust so team members know that you remain reliable, trustworthy, and committed to program priorities and steps along the path. Your follow-up models for teachers what you want them to do with colleagues, families, and children, and demonstrates what earning and maintaining trust looks like. It moves the work along and conveys the belief that the team advances the work together.

Here are few additional tips for following up after team meetings:

- **Distribute notes to the team.** Ensure that they are clear, brief, and capture key ideas, decisions, and next steps.

    - Include something you or a participant noticed about the group's moment(s) of effectiveness and why it mattered to the team's learning.

    - Communicate plans for the next convening, including date, time, location, and key agenda items.

- **Send the meeting notes as soon as possible after the meeting.** This helps team members to see that their collaboration during the meeting matters in their day-to-day work. It reminds everyone of team decisions and next steps and promotes ownership.

- **Recall individual team members' contributions when you see them after the meeting.** When you see or interact with individuals after the meeting, tell them that you noticed and value a specific comment, question, or support they offered a colleague, articulating why the contribution matters for the group's process further validates them as partners in the team's learning and work together. This also builds motivation to both follow through and be an active learning partner.

- **Just prior to the next convening, send a reminder notice**. Include the agenda and specific prompts/questions for the group to be prepared to discuss. Then the effective, productive, and satisfying team meeting cycle continues.

In this chapter we described many different facets of the 'how' of team meetings: what you and the group will do before, during, and after meetings. We're guessing this was a lot to digest. Go slow. Try a little bit each time. Introduce new strategies little by little. Appreciate small steps and recognize that change takes time. In the next chapter, we offer a few ideas for facilitating team meetings.

CHAPTER 5
FACILITATING TEAM MEETINGS — THE LEADING FOR CHILDREN WAY

At Leading for Children, we use facilitation to change power dynamics and create space for all voices to be heard. In this way we allow the wisdom of the group to be the foundation for thinking, problem-solving, and learning. As articulated in the opening of the guide, when we elevate the *wisdom* of the group, we strengthen *teams*, and use practices in team meetings that *model* best practices for children. The chapter covers your facilitative stance and facilitation strategies. It focuses on what you do during team meetings to value and support all team members as they share their knowledge and learn new ways to be effective in their work.

YOUR FACILITATIVE STANCE

Your stance is your attitudes, thoughts and feelings that guide your actions and words.

A Facilitative Stance

The dictionary definition of facilitation is helping to bring about an outcome (such as learning, productivity, or communication) by providing indirect or unobtrusive assistance, guidance, or supervision. An effective early learning teacher provides an environment, experiences, and interactions that encourage children to be curious investigators. This approach allows children to think flexibly and interact effectively with materials and people. Have you heard the expression — *rather than sage on the stage, the teacher is the guide on the side*? Effective leaders use a parallel facilitation process with teachers. What you do and how you are with them is the way you want them to be in their parallel day-to-day work with children and families. Author and educator, Maria Nichols, writes about teachers use of a facilitative stance to encourage children's honest flow of talk and meaning making.[8]

Facilitators invite inquiry and engagement and encourage reflection. When team meeting participants know they are seen and heard for the wisdom they bring, they feel a sense of belonging and connection and are more likely to fully engage with their colleagues. Similarly, when adults help children to experience a sense of belonging and validation, there is trust and openness to learn. Children can see themselves as part of a community of thinkers and learners with something valuable to contribute.

In one analogy facilitators are viewed as air traffic controllers, not pilots. Pilots are experts at flying planes. Air traffic controllers provide direction and coordination for planes to get where they are going as easily and safely as possible. When a group forms for any reason, people move at different speeds and directions. As a facilitator, it's not your job to be the expert on every topic, know the answer to every question, or figure out how everyone should contribute. Instead, you establish a trusting environment so each person can do that for themselves and for their fellow participants.

TEAM LEADERS
ON FACILITATION

The word facilitator sticks with me because sometimes I barrel on ahead to make sure I get everything in that teachers need to know. And really, I should be facilitating conversation and learning.
— Anne, Preschool Program Director

Facilitating means bringing everybody's voice in the room, not getting through an agenda. To walk hand-in-hand down the path forward. To give people time to think. If you hurry, somebody's voice is going to become invisible.
— Devora, Early Childhood Program Director

Facilitation is knowing that we can build more authentic learning together as a group of co-learners, than a 'presenter' could alone. It is we not me. It is modeling the best practices for early childhood teaching: guiding learning with intentional questions and building relationships.
— Early Learning Program Leader

---

[8] M. Nichols, "Building bigger ideas: A process for teaching purposeful talk." Last modified January 22, 2019. https://readingrecovery.org/who-owns-the-learning-the-importance-of-adopting-a-facilitative-stance/.

Facilitation Strategies

Facilitation is as much a state of mind as it is a set of strategies. If you genuinely believe in the wisdom of the group and trust the process, your team will be engaged. As with everything in life, patience matters. You might be introducing a new approach to team meetings, thereby changing a paradigm. Many of us, including the program team, may have had years of experience passively sitting in meetings where we are told what we should know and what we have to do. Change takes time. Some team members will get on board right away because they see the advantages of the new approach. Others may be curious while not ready to jump in and one or more may be skeptical of anything new.

Facilitation is the act of engaging participants in creating, discovering, and applying insights. In contrast to presentation, which is typically characterized by a "sage on the stage" delivering content to an audience, the facilitator asks questions, moderates discussions, introduces activities, and helps participants learn. Rather than reading from PowerPoint slides, the facilitator shares content with participants by:

- Offering a prompt and inviting discussion
- Using articles, blog posts, and quotes to read and discuss
- Providing hands-on experiences so that group members can explore and solve problems

Tips for Effective Facilitation

Here are some ideas that help to foster interactions and deep thinking organized into three categories: How you affect the group's experience, how to be inclusive, and how to stay focused on the goals of the meeting.

Be a role model for strong positive relationships and a feeling of community.

Relationships are central to our work as educators and nurturing relationships is one of *The Five Commitments of Optimistic Leaders*.

Pay attention to language.

Language can be subtle or direct, received as intended or misinterpreted, clear or confusing. Consider the impact of your communication and make sure the messages you convey have the intended meaning. Wherever possible, be invitational rather than demanding. Convey that the individual is the decision maker and has choice. For example, instead of saying:

- What I need you to do next is…try saying, *I invite you to think about…*

- Who can tell me a strategy you use for family engagement?…try saying, *Let's think about the many ways you engage with families.*

Focus on questions rather than answers. Plan to ask several open-ended questions that invite inquiry and expansive thinking. Use prompts and questions that generate diverse perspectives. For example:

- What are some ways we already help children form friendships?

- Think about children who have temperaments different from yours. How do you begin to find out what strategies for friendship making would work for them?

- How can we engage families in supporting their children's friendships?

- Where else can we learn more about children and friendships?

Model activating curiosity in response to individual contributions. This helps you to suspend judgement in response to an individual's idea, belief, question, or stance that clashes with your own. In addition, you will be modelling the strategy for the group. Asking reflective questions from a stance of curiosity helps you and the group to listen to learn rather than listening to respond or react negatively. "What might happen if…?

Promote inclusivity.

Your team will feel validated and included when they are seen and heard. Be sure to include all voices in meetings by ensuring participation from everyone, including those who may not be comfortable speaking in a group. Some people speak more often than others and some people are reluctant to speak, ever. Insisting that people speak is disrespectful, but these strategies are often helpful.

Use Carousel Share to hear all voices. Offer a question or a prompt related to the topic. You could offer a prompt related to the topic. For example, if the topic of the meeting is preparation for upcoming family conferences, you might say: *"Take a moment to think about a word or phrase that captures how you want families to feel when they leave the conference for their child."* Invite everyone to take a moment or two to think and jot down a few words or phrases on a post-it to remember their main idea. Then, ask each member of the group to read what she or he wrote without elaboration. Remind the group to take notes as each person shares. There is no back and forth conversation between each share. After everyone has offered an idea, you, or a participant, can lead a brief discussion about common themes heard.

Use the think, pair, share strategy. Individuals turn to a partner and share their idea. After everyone has had a chance to rehearse expressing their thinking, you can invite volunteers to share something they said or heard.

Set expectations for speaking up. You might say:

- Talk with your table group and decide together on one idea to share. Then we'll hear from each table group.

- Let's hear four different perspectives on this topic.

Offer people choice. In an effort to include all voices, resist the urge to hear from everyone or to insist that each person take a turn. For example, you might offer a prompt with this caveat: "Think about something that happened this week that you are feeling optimistic about. Take a moment to recall your experience and then jot it down. I'll invite everyone to share what they have written. You can choose to pass or ask us to return to you later in the conversation."

Form discussion groups of three to four people. Not everyone is comfortable speaking up in a large group and too often the same voices do most of the talking. Vary group sizes and mix groups so that different people have a chance to interact with one another.

Encourage participants to engage with each other. Typically, when a group member asks a question or responds to a prompt from the facilitator, the person talks to the facilitator. Invite the person speaking to "aim" towards the center of the room or to a person at the other side of the room. This models an action that effective teachers do with children. That ideas shared are to the group with the intention that everyone is listening, and that every voice is respected.

Navigate dominant voices. There are times when a participant goes on and on, even after you have provided coaching related to the behavior. Because it feels impolite to interrupt someone, you may be reluctant to step in, but the rest of the group is relying on you! When the person takes a breath, you might try what feels the most comfortable for you:

- Say "Thank you."
- Summarize the speaker's statement.
- Note that there are others waiting to speak.
- Walk closer to the person speaking.
- Give a "wrap up" sign with your hands.
- Say, "Please wind down your idea."
- Write their idea up on the flipchart and ask, "Have I got that right here?"
- Say "Thank you Patty, we need to move on, are there any other comments?"

Appreciate silence. Be aware of your own comfort with silence. We all need time to think and this is absolutely something we want to model for working with children, so we must do it with adults. If you ask a question and nobody answers, avoid answering it yourself. You want to set an expectation for dialogue, not monologue, so give it the space to happen. Some language you might use includes:

- "I can tell you're really thinking, I'll pause a little longer before we start our conversation."
- "Hmm…would it be easier to have this conversation at your table?"
- "Maybe we can table this question for our next meeting."

Include storytelling. Meetings become moments of connection when people recall personal stories and draw out insights. Stories also help people with perspective taking. Offer a prompt and invite the person next to you to share a brief story. Invite pairs to think together about common elements of their stories. To debrief, invite insights from stories that relate to the topic. Encourage people to listen without interrupting.

Facilitating Team Meetings — The Leading for Children Way

Stay focused on the goals of the meeting.

Many people have asked how to have inclusive conversations and still make sure you address the goals of the meeting. When planning the agenda, you thought carefully about how much time to allocate for each segment. Stay present and focused as you guide the meeting.

Manage side issues or less relevant thoughts and questions respectfully and constructively. If someone raises an issue that is not relevant to the topic, use a "parking lot." This is a chart with post-it notes that allows you to honor the idea's importance. You can say that the topic matters and can be addressed at another time. This reassures people that their concerns and ideas matter and models the same responsiveness you want them to practice with children.

Be flexible and ready to adjust the plan. Unanticipated issues, dynamics, ideas, and questions may arise. Model responsiveness as the discussion evolves. Some topics or processes may require more time than is available or need a different group thinking strategy. Be transparent about adjustments you make, continuing to link them to the meeting purpose and main ideas, and checking in with the group for agreement.

Read the group continually in order to be a responsive facilitator. Pay attention to words, body language, and signs of agreement/disagreement. This is important for promoting mutual clarity and understanding and assuring everyone that this is a safe space for sharing, asking questions, and solving problems.

Ensure a logical flow and smooth transitions between agenda items. Consider how the segments of the meeting can build upon each other and allow for smooth and clear transitions. Weave connections from one segment to the next throughout the meeting to scaffold the participants' deepening of their understanding of the key messages and outcomes.

Encourage charting to synthesize ideas. Very often in meetings people talk and at the end of the conversation, it is hard for them to remember key ideas. Using chart paper and markers with an assignment of what to document ensures that the group has a focus and can then share what they discussed with others in the room.

Take a gallery walk. As an alternative to whole group sharing of charts, have each group hang their charts on the walls. Provide a few minutes for everyone to review the charts, noticing similarities and differences, common themes, and new ideas. If new strategies are generated on charts, we will often suggest that people take photos to have a record of the strategy.

REMOTE MEETINGS
GALLERY WALKS

If you have some members who will be attending a meeting via video conference, be sure to allow them to view charts and participate in gallery walk activities. If charts cannot be shown on camera, one lower-tech solution is to have a note-taker record what is being charted and share their screen with remote participants.

Using a facilitative stance encourages team to think, problem-solve, and learn together. Often participants gain a sense of power and self-esteem that carries back to the classroom. When you model how to promote healthy relationships and interactions in safe and nurturing environments, team members can mirror your words and actions in their work with children, families, and colleagues.

NEXT STEPS

You have reached the end of this guide, *Effective Team Meetings: An Optimistic Leader's Guide*, and hopefully, you have many ideas you might try. Consider reflecting on your team meetings, identifying what is working well and a few strategies you want to try out first. Too often we try to tackle too much and that can be discouraging. The reflection questions below encourage you to build on the effectiveness of your meetings and to set reasonable goals for enhancing them.

Think about your current team meeting practices (planning, implementing, and following up).

What is working well? Why do you think so?

1.

2.

3.

As you think about meeting practices you would like to improve, what are you ready to try first?

1.

2.

3.

If you have identified a few long-term goals, note them here so that you can come back to them as you become more comfortable implementing a more facilitative stance.

1

2

3

ACTION PLAN

Consider creating a plan for applying the lessons learned and trying out a few strategies at a time. This Action Plan framework can serve as a tool for recording what is important to you and deciding what you want to do next. Think about a specific aspect of your team meetings. Note what you are already doing and what you want to try. Reflect on how this aspect of your meetings aligns with the mission, vision, culture and climate of your program. Then, think about the Five Commitments of Optimistic Leadership and the Coherent Path to Quality. What alignment do you see there? And, how might you enhance what you are doing to garner more alignment?

An example is provided below to illustrate how you might use the action plan.

Focus: Choosing Topics

WHAT WE DO NOW	We have weekly staff meetings. Mostly my associate director and I come up with topics based on what is going on week by week.
WHAT WE COULD TRY	I want to establish a staff meeting planning committee to think about an overall plan for topics for each quarter of the year.
ALIGNMENT WITH MISSION, VISION, CULTURE, AND CLIMATE	The committee will review the mission and vision of the school and think about how to make sure our topics are aligned.
ALIGNMENT WITH THE FIVE COMMITMENTS AND THE COHERENT PATH	I like the idea of using The Five Commitments as group norms. An initial topic will be to review them and think together about how group norms can support us having more productive meetings.

Reflections

Describe what happened when you implemented this change.

Record the responses of the team to this change.

What else might you do related to this focus?

Focus: _____

WHAT WE DO NOW	
WHAT WE COULD TRY	
ALIGNMENT WITH MISSION, VISION, CULTURE, AND CLIMATE	
ALIGNMENT WITH THE FIVE COMMITMENTS AND THE COHERENT PATH	

ACKNOWLEDGEMENTS

I love having thought partners — it is one of life's greatest pleasures. The guide began by meeting with the Development Collaborative, a group of amazing educators: Mimi Basso, Amy Warden, Jeannette Corey, Joan Kuo, Jackie Klein, Laura Ensler, Monica McCarthy, and Nichole Parks. Gratitude to each of you for the wisdom you shared as we thought together about how to transform staff meetings into professional learning conversations. My LFC colleagues, Nichole Parks and Laura Ensler, have partnered with me to define Leading for Children's facilitation strategies. Amy Dombro, my writing partner and champion of many years, helped me organize an early draft of this guide. Derry Koralek helped me get the manuscript into shape with her wisdom and clarity. Michael Luft, Diana Courson, Jill Gunderman, and Monica McCarthy influenced my thinking about how to ensure that group conversations are two-way. Without the persistent encouragement of Gretchen Henderson, Lisa Holton, and Gary Romano, this guide would still be in my head. Thanks also to Emily Ropers and Ann Kremer in Illinois for inviting me to work remotely with preschool special education leaders in Illinois. Together we learned a great deal about making meetings inclusive and dynamic. Tara Skiles, you are an amazing thought partner and I have so much appreciation for the conversations we have together and for the opportunity to work with the excellent educators in Alabama. Diana Courson, a special thanks to you for giving me so many rich opportunities to facilitate group conversations with early learning educators across Arkansas. Shelli Aiona Kim and Sandy Lighter-Jones, the work we did together at Kamehameha in Hawaii set me on the path to begin Leading for Children. Thanks to Erin Murphy for making the guide beautiful. And finally, to our many donors who have supported Leading for Children since we began in 2016, thank you so much for your generous contributions that helped to make this resource possible.